5-1-03

Dear Janet —

You love to cook
to nourish others, so
this little book is for
you. I hope you
enjoy these recipes.

Like good yeast,
may GOD's love continue
to grow in your heart
and spill over to bless
many, many others.

Love Always
and forever —
mom

An Amish Table

An Amish Table

Phyllis Pellman Good

Good Books

Intercourse, PA 17534
800/762-7171
www.goodbks.com

Cover photos by Jerry Irwin and Jonathan Charles.
Other photography by Jonathan Charles, Doyle Yoder, and David Lauver.
Design by Dawn J. Ranck

AN AMISH TABLE
Copyright © 1994 by Good Books, Intercourse, Pennsylvania 17534
Printed in China
International Standard Book Number: 1-56148-130-0
Library of Congress Catalog Card Number: 94-33292

Library of Congress Cataloging-in-Publication Data
Good, Phyllis Pellman, 1948-
    An Amish table / Phyllis Pellman Good.
        p. cm.
    ISBN 1-56148-130-0
    1. Cookery, Amish. I. Title.
TX715.G61725   1994
641.5'66--dc20
                                                                94-33292
                                                                CIP

An Introduction

The Amish have captured the interest of the modern world because of their quaint clothing, horses and buggies, their striking quilts, their lusty food. These people prefer to be regarded as a community of faith who deliberately seek to live in a way that honors God and the creation.

How did the Amish develop and retain a food tradition that is identifiable? With their sustained rural base, the Amish have maintained a productive relationship with their gardens and fields. With their large extended families they have not only been able to convey the love of certain dishes to their children, but they have also been able to show their daughters how to make those specialties, many of which are learned best by "feel" rather than by reading a cookbook. In addition, their active community life supports the continuation of a food tradition—at gathered times, favorite dishes appear, undergirding the event, whether it be a school picnic, a funeral, or sisters' day.

An Amish Table contains old recipes, but they are written to be understood and used by those without the benefit of these people's history or the presence of an experienced cook. Here, then, is the possibility of making good food—not fancy, but substantial; more hearty than delicate; in tune with the seasons.

Chicken Roast

Roast is a crowd pleaser. Today it is the main dish served at Old Order Amish weddings in Lancaster County. It has been so for many years.

Some families make roast for Christmas dinner. Others traditionally prepared it for threshers.

Roast has the qualifications for being a favorite in the Amish community for cook and feasters alike. Its ingredients are readily available; the combination of flavors is basic and full-bodied; it can be prepared with turkey or duck if the supply—or taste preferences of those eating—so demand.

1½ loaves homemade bread	1 tsp. celery seed
1 lb. butter or margarine	¾ cup celery, chopped (optional)
1½ tsp. salt	meat from a whole chicken, stewed
½ tsp. pepper	and removed from bones

Crumble the bread by hand into a large mixing bowl. Melt the butter; then pour it over the bread crumbs. Add the seasonings and chopped celery. Then mix with the deboned chicken chunks.

Turn into a large roast pan and bake covered at 350° for a half hour to an hour, until heated through. Dampen with water around the edge if it begins to dry out. Stir often to prevent sticking.

Note: You may make a rich gravy to serve over the roast by thickening the chicken broth with flour.

Homemade Noodles

Makes 1 pound

Noodles became a specialty of the German settlers in Pennsylvania. They brought with them a taste for the dish. It was in the rich farmland of the mid-Atlantic area of the New World, however, that wheat flourished as it hadn't in Europe. Here the people had access to wheat flour. Many farms also had their own flocks of chickens and, thus, the eggs needed to make the rich dough.

One Amish woman in her early 40s explains, "Having your own eggs makes it easier to make your own noodles and pot pie. A lot of the older people want noodles at the main meal each day because they used to make them weekly." An older man agrees, "We always had homemade noodles. Some places today they don't have any chickens—they have big dairies instead—so they have to buy their noodles."

In some families, noodlemaking had a seasonal aspect. One woman, born in the 1920s, recalls, "If we had a lot of eggs, we'd make a lot of noodles. In the spring, when the chickens were older, the egg shells weren't as strong, so we'd have many 'cracks.' Then we'd mix up noodles, using the egg yolks. I would come home from school and see the noodles drying. I knew that somewhere there were egg whites waiting to be made into chocolate angel food cake!"

Today's cooks need to weigh the matchless flavor of homemade noodles, yet the heavy time investment they require, against the inexpensive store-bought noodles that are so easily had. In most Amish homes, made-from-scratch noodles are a treat, rather then a regularly served dish.

6 eggs yolks	**3 cups flour (approximately)**
6 Tbsp. water	**½ tsp. salt**

Beat the egg yolks and water together thoroughly. Stir in the salt and flour to make a very stiff, yet workable dough.

Divide the dough into four balls. Roll each one out, making as thin a layer as possible. Lay each on a separate cloth to dry.

When they are dry enough not to stick together, stack them on top of each other and cut them lengthwise into thin strips. Then cut across the width of the dough to form thin strips, about 1½-2 inches long.

Allow noodles to dry completely before storing them in an airtight container.

To Serve Homemade Noodles:

Bring 3 quarts of water to a boil. Add 1½ Tbsp. salt and ½ lb. homemade noodles. Stir frequently. After water returns to boil, cook for 8-10 minutes. Drain and serve, covered with brown butter.

Note: Brown butter is a simple, yet pleasing topping for cooked noodles. It is a tradition practiced widely by Amish cooks, especially for use with noodles and steamed vegetables.

Melt desired amount of butter in saucepan. Allow it to brown (watch carefully so it doesn't burn). Pour over noodles in their serving dish.

Oyster Pie

"Oyster pie was always a treat, although we had it maybe once a month. An oyster man came around regularly, and he'd give a lot more juice with the oysters than you get in the store!"

Only sixty miles from Philadelphia, the Lancaster area had easy access to the fish and oyster trade flowing through the seaport city. In fact, Lancaster farmers sold their wheat, which they raised primarily as a cash crop during the mid to late 1800s, in Philadelphia. Or they took their potatoes to Reading where, by way of the canal system, they were sent on to Philadelphia. In addition to seafood, lemons, oranges, and bananas found their way to Lancaster tables.

4 cups potatoes, cooked and cubed	1 tsp. salt
¼ cup celery, chopped	¼ tsp. pepper
1 pint oysters with liquor	2 Tbsp. butter
2 eggs, hardboiled and cut up	1½ cups milk

Alternate layers of potatoes, celery, oysters, eggs, and seasonings in baking pan. Dot with butter. Pour milk and oyster liquid over.

Crust

1½ cups flour	1 egg, beaten
½ tsp. salt	2 Tbsp. cold water
½ cup plus 2 Tbsp. shortening	1½ tsp. vinegar

Mix flour and salt. Cut in shortening.

Combine egg, water, and vinegar and stir into shortening mixture. Refrigerate for a few minutes.

Roll out dough on floured board. Place over oyster mixture. Cut slits in dough to permit steam to escape. Bake at 375° for 45 minutes.

Beef Roast

When canning was perfected in the late 19th century, many Amish cooks found that process to be the solution to having meat with a fresh—rather than smoked—flavor, year-round. Until then, fresh meat was stored either under fat in the cellar or in the cool springhouse. Recalls one woman, "We had a big water trough in our pantry that was spring-fed. It was as long as a bathtub, and we used that to cool food."

Canning took away the pressure to use meat quickly before it spoiled. It provided the cook, too, with the prospect of a nearly instant meal, should drop-in company appear or other duties keep her preoccupied. Many Amish cooks still can meat since they are able to store it at home, in the absence of home freezers.

As important as preparing flavorful and tender meat is creating a good gravy. The cook, whether using fresh or canned meat, intends to have a rich broth to work with when the meat is finished cooking.

For roast with bone, allow ⅓ lb. per serving. For boneless roast, allow ¼ lb. per serving.

beef roast	**water**
salt and pepper to taste	**salt and pepper to taste**
water	
flour (use 2½ Tbsp. for each cup of water added after meat is finished roasting)	

Season roast on all sides with salt and pepper. Place in roast pan and add about ½ inch of water. Cover. Roast at 325°, allowing about 30 minutes per pound if the cut is a high quality (rib roast, for example); about 50-60 minutes per pound if the cut is less tender (a chuck or rump roast, for example).

When meat is tender, remove it from the roasting pan.

Mix or shake flour and additional water together until all lumps are gone. Stir into roast drippings in pan over low heat on top of the stove, until it comes to a boil and thickens slightly into a gravy. Taste and add more salt and pepper if needed.

Slice meat onto platter, pour gravy into boat, and serve.

Tomato Soup with Celery, Peppers, and Carrots

Makes 3 servings

Some Amish cooks can a pulpy tomato juice, so laden with vegetables that their tomato soup requires no additional thickening.

1 pint tomato juice cocktail	$\frac{1}{8}$ tsp. baking soda
scant $\frac{1}{4}$ cup water	$\frac{1}{4}$ cup milk
("Just enough to rinse out the jar!")	

Heat juice and water to the boiling point. Stir soda in carefully, watching that the mixture doesn't boil over.

Add milk and heat, but don't boil.

Tomato Juice Cocktail

$\frac{1}{2}$ bushel tomatoes	3 green peppers
3 stalks celery (leaves and all)	a little water
3 large onions	1 cup sugar
6 medium carrots	2 Tbsp. salt

Cut raw vegetables into 1-inch pieces. Put all together into large stockpot. Add water to a depth of 1 inch. Cook slowly until soft, then put through food press.

To puréed mixture add sugar and salt. Bring to a boil. Pour into jars and seal.

Chicken Corn Soup

Makes 8-10 servings

Chicken and corn have unusually compatible flavors. This soup is a newer twist on the traditional pot pie. With the addition of noodles or rivvels it has a close resemblance to, yet is a welcome variation of, the old favorite. Again, the ingredients are homegrown.

Amish cooks are sought after to prepare the Chicken Corn Soup offered for lunch at local fire company dinners and at the food stands at farm auctions in the Lancaster area.

3-4 lbs. stewing chicken	rivvels (optional)
salt to taste	3-4 hard-boiled eggs, diced (optional)
water	dash of pepper
2 quarts corn, fresh, frozen, or canned	

In large kettle, cover chicken pieces with water. Salt to taste. Cook until tender, then cut meat off bones and dice into bite-sized pieces.

Return chicken to broth. Add corn and bring to a boil. Stir in rivvels or hard-boiled eggs and cook until rivvels are cooked through. Add pepper and serve.

Rivvels

¾ **cup flour**
1 egg

Put flour in bowl. Break in egg and mix with a fork until dry and crumbly.

Baked Corn

Makes 6 servings

Corn, fresh or canned, can be made into a pleasing custard. Eggs and milk are still plentiful on most Amish homesteads.

2 cups corn	**$\frac{1}{2}$ tsp. salt**
2 eggs	**dash of pepper**
1 cup milk	**2 Tbsp. melted butter or margarine**
1 Tbsp. flour	**$\frac{1}{2}$ cup bread or cracker crumbs**
1 Tbsp. sugar, optional	**2 Tbsp. butter or margarine**

Cook the corn. Beat the eggs and milk. Combine corn, eggs and milk, flour, seasonings, and 2 Tbsp. butter or margarine. Mix well.

Pour into greased 1½-quart baking dish. Mix crumbs and butter and sprinkle over corn. Bake at 350° for 40 minutes or until mixture is set.

Corn Pie

Here, corn in combination with potatoes makes a meal. Add chicken chunks and you have an adaptation of chicken pot pie.

Pastry for a 2-crust pie
3 cups fresh corn
1½ cups raw potatoes, diced
2 or 3 hard-boiled eggs, diced

salt and pepper to taste
2 Tbsp. flour
milk

Line a casserole or deep pie pan with pastry.

Combine corn, potatoes, and eggs and pour into pastry-lined container. Add salt and pepper. Sprinkle with flour. Add enough milk to cover the vegetables.

Cover with top pastry. Pinch edges together to seal.

Bake at 425° for 30-40 minutes, until crust is browned and milk is bubbly throughout.

Variation: Add chunks of chicken, cut into 1" pieces.

Tomato Gravy

Tomatoes last into cornhusking time in the fall. One Amish grandmother has warm memories of both her mother and grandmother fixing tomato gravy to ladle over fried potatoes. It was their welcome for those who had spent cool fall evenings in the fields.

> **1 quart peeled tomato slices or canned tomatoes**
> **3 Tbsp. flour**
> **2-3 Tbsp. water**
> **4 Tbsp. brown sugar**

Heat tomatoes slowly until they reach the boiling point. Meanwhile, stir flour and water together until smooth.

When tomatoes come to a boil, add flour-water paste and sugar, stirring until the gravy thickens. Eat over fried potatoes or toast.

New Potatoes and Peas

Makes 4-6 servings

This is a springtime feast. Some cooks favor only a brown butter dressing; others prefer a white sauce.

New potatoes may be cooked in their papery skins, or they may be gently scraped with a knife (not a potato peeler) so that only the thin shell is removed.

12 small new potatoes
3 cups fresh peas
1 tsp. salt
brown butter or a white sauce

Cook potatoes in a small amount of water until almost soft. Add peas and cook just until they and the potatoes are tender. Salt.

Spoon into serving dish and pour brown butter or white sauce over.

White Sauce

2 Tbsp. butter or margarine
1½ tsp. flour
1½ cups milk

Melt butter or margarine. Stir in flour to form paste. Gradually add milk, stirring constantly over heat until smooth and thickened.

Cucumbers and Onions

Makes 4-6 servings

2 medium cucumbers	1 Tbsp. sugar
2 medium onions	1 Tbsp. vinegar
salt	
2-3 Tbsp. mayonnaise or salad dressing	

Peel cucumbers and slice thin. Layer in shallow dish, sprinkling each layer with salt. Let stand overnight.

In the morning, drain cucumbers and rinse. Let dry on paper towels.

Slice onions thin. Mix gently with cucumber slices.

Beat together the mayonnaise or salad dressing, sugar, and vinegar until creamy. Stir into mixed cucumbers and onions. (The dressing should be plentiful so the salad is creamy. Increase amounts of dressing ingredients, proportionally, if needed.)

Chow Chow

This canning project works well in late summer as gardening begins to wind down. Chow chow does not require the youngest, tiniest vegetables, so it is a way to use the last of the season's yield.

In some families, sisters get together for chow-chow making. That relieves the tedium of chopping and cooking the numerous vegetables that go into the most subtly flavored, variously textured, and brightly colored chow chow.

4 cups lima beans	4 cups cucumbers, cut in chunks
4 cups green string beans	4 cups corn kernels
2 cups yellow wax beans	4 cups granulated sugar
4 cups cabbage, chopped	3 cups apple cider vinegar
4 cups cauliflower florets	1 cup water
4 cups carrots, sliced	1 Tbsp. pickling spices
4 cups celery, cut in chunks	1 Tbsp. mustard seed
4 cups red and green peppers, chopped	1 Tbsp. celery seed
4 cups small white onions	

Cook each vegetable separately until tender but not mushy. When each is finished, lift out of hot water with a slotted spoon and rinse with cold water to stop its cooking and preserve its color. Drain, then layer into a large dishpan.

Combine the sugar, vinegar, water, and spices in a 15-quart stockpot (or do half a batch at a time in an 8-quart kettle) and bring to a boil. Make sure the sugar is fully dissolved, then spoon all the vegetables (or half of them, depending upon the size of the kettle) into the syrup and boil for 5 minutes. Stir gently, only to mix the vegetables well.

Spoon into hot sterilized jars and seal.

Ham and Green Beans

Smoked hams hung in the attic from one fall's butchering until the next. When the supply was strong, ham and green beans could be made with a smoked shoulder or picnic. As the number and size of the meat cuts dwindled, ham and green beans could still be made, although it was more likely prepared with a ham butt, primarily for flavoring.

Green beans were dried, and in later years canned, for use throughout the winter months, and so this dish developed as a sort of tasty and logical combination. The unnamed, but expected ingredient in this meal was potatoes, often cut up in chunks rather than mashed.

A customary side dish was cole slaw. Its vinegar dressing provided the "bite" to offset the heavier meat. Furthermore, cabbage kept well into the spring and so was handy for this wintry meal.

Although much time had already been spent in butchering and curing the ham, in picking and preserving the green beans, and in digging the potatoes, the immediate preparation of this meal was relatively quick and easy for the cook.

2-3 lb. ham shoulder or picnic, or 1-2 lb. ham hock
4 potatoes, peeled and cut in chunks
1 quart green beans

Place the ham in a roaster, add ½ cup water and cover. Bake at 350° for 1-1½ hours.

Add potatoes and green beans to roaster. Cover and return to oven for an additional hour of baking.

This can also be cooked on top of the stove. Place the ham in a heavy kettle. Add 2 inches of water and cook slowly, covered, for 1½ hours. Add potatoes and green beans and continue cooking slowly for another hour, or until the meat is tender and the potatoes are soft.

Pickled Red Beets

20 medium-sized red beets
2½ cups apple cider vinegar
2½ cups beet juice
1 cup granulated sugar

2 tsp. salt
10 whole cloves
2 cinnamon sticks

Scrub beets and remove tops. Cook beets until tender. Drain and reserve beet juice. Remove skins and cut beets into chunks.

Combine vinegar, juice, sugar, and spices. Bring to a boil. Remove spices. Add beet chunks and boil again. Pour into hot sterilized jars and seal.

Red Beet Eggs

6 hard-boiled eggs, peeled
2½ cups leftover sweet and sour red beet juice syrup

Pour cool syrup over cooked and peeled eggs. Let stand overnight in refrigerator. To serve, slice the eggs in half, lengthwise.

Potato Bread

Makes 3 loaves

3½ cups milk
6 Tbsp. sugar
6 Tbsp. butter
2 tsp. salt
½ cup mashed potatoes

2 packages dry yeast
½ cup lukewarm water
3 cups whole wheat flour
7-8 cups white flour

Scald milk. Add sugar, butter, salt, and mashed potatoes. Cool to lukewarm.
Meanwhile, dissolve yeast in water. Add to cooled milk mixture.

Add whole wheat flour and 1 cup white flour. Beat 2 minutes with mixer. Stir in
6-7 more cups flour until dough leaves sides of bowl.

Turn onto lightly floured surface. Knead gently until dough forms a smooth ball.
Place in greased bowl. Turn once to grease top of dough. Cover and let rise in a warm
place away from drafts until double, 1½-2 hours. Punch down and let rise again until
double.

Turn onto floured surface and divide dough into 3 equal parts. Cover and let rest
10 minutes.

Form into 3 loaves and place in greased bread pans.

Bake at 350° for 40-45 minutes. Remove from pans and place on rack to cool.

Sticky Buns

Makes 2 dozen

These breakfast favorites are also commonly known as Sweet Rolls, Cinnamon Rolls, or Pecan Stickies. The basic sweet roll dough adapts easily to varied glazes and fillings.

These buns have made satisfying snacks before the late afternoon milking. They also pack well into school lunch boxes.

1 package dry yeast	1 tsp. salt
1/4 cup warm water	1 egg beaten
1/4 cup shortening	3 1/4-4 cups flour
1/4 cup sugar	
1 cup milk, scalded, or 1 cup warm water	

Dissolve yeast in warm water.

In large bowl, cream shortening and sugar. Pour hot milk or water over mixture. Cool to lukewarm. Add 1 cup flour and beat well. Beat in yeast mixture and egg.

Gradually add remaining flour to form a soft dough, beating well.

Brush top of dough with softened margarine or butter. Cover and let rise in warm place until double (1 1/2-2 hours).

Punch down and knead. Form rolls. Let rise again until doubled. Bake according to instructions on the following page.

For Cinnamon Rolls:

Divide dough in half. Roll each half into a rectangle, approximately 12" x 8". Spread with butter and sprinkle with a mixture of ½ cup brown sugar and 1 tsp. cinnamon. Roll as a jelly roll. Cut into 1-1½" slices. Place rolls in greased pans about ¾" apart. Let rise and bake at 350° for 30 minutes. Cool and spread with doughnut glaze.

Doughnut Glaze

1 lb. 10x sugar	1 Tbsp. soft butter
½ cup rich milk (or a bit more)	1 tsp. vanilla

Heat together just until butter is melted and milk is warm. Glaze while doughnuts are hot.

For Raisin Cinnamon Rolls:

Make rolls as above, but sprinkle with raisins before rolling up. Bake as above.

For Pecan Stickies:

Place ½ cup pecans in bottom of each of two greased 9½" x 5" x 3" pans. Make syrup by heating slowly: ½ cup brown sugar, ¼ cup butter, and 1 Tbsp. light corn syrup. Pour half of syrup over each pan of pecans. Prepare Cinnamon Rolls, using only ¼ cup brown sugar, and place rolls on top of pecans and syrup.

Let rise till double and bake at 375° for about 25 minutes. Remove from oven and turn pan upside down onto a flat plate.

Syrup will run down through the rolls and pecans will be on top.

Half-Moon Pies

Makes 2-2½ dozen individual pies

A variation on schnitz pie developed in the Big Valley area of Pennsylvania, where an Amish settlement began in 1790. The Amish, who live west and south of Lewistown in the central part of the state, fashioned a schnitz pie that travels well—in the hand or in lunch boxes! Its name is descriptive of how the finished delicacy looks.

2 quarts dried apples	¾ tsp. cinnamon
3 cups water	1½ tsp. allspice
1½ cups granulated sugar	¾ tsp. salt
1½ cups brown sugar	pie dough for 4 9"-shells

Boil the dried apples in the water until the water is fully absorbed.

While they are cooking, prepare the pie dough. Then drain the apples. Blend in sugar and spices.

To form the individual pies, take a piece of dough about the size of an egg and shape it into a ball. Roll out into a circle until the dough is thin, yet able to hold the filling. Fold dough in half to form a crease through the center. Unfold.

Mark the top of one half with a pie crimper to shape the rounded edge. Put ½ cup of the schnitz filling on the other half. Wet the outer edges of the dough. Fold the marked half over the half with the filling. Press edges together, cutting off ragged edges with the pie crimper.

Brush the tops with beaten egg, lift onto cookie sheets, and bake at 425° until golden brown.

Shoofly Pie

Makes 1 9" pie

This cakey pie, with a name that has produced a myriad of explanations for its existence, may have its roots in the early bakeovens of Pennsylvania. Dense cakes with heavy dough were put into the bakeovens following the weekly bread-baking, which required the hottest fires. This hybrid cake within a pie shell weathered the bakeoven well. It was with the advent of the kitchen range and its more easily controlled temperatures that lighter pies with custards, creams, and more delicate fruit became common.

Crumbs

1 cup flour
⅔ cup light brown sugar

1 Tbsp. shortening

Mix flour and sugar. Cut in shortening. Take out ½ cup crumbs and set aside.

Bottom Part

1 egg, slightly beaten
1 cup molasses
1 cup boiling water

1 tsp. baking soda
1 9" unbaked pie shell

To larger portion of crumb mixture add egg and molasses. Blend in ¾ cup boiling water. Dissolve soda in remaining ¼ cup water and add last.

Pour into unbaked pie shell. Sprinkle reserved crumbs on top. Bake at 425° for 15 minutes. Reduce heat to 350° and bake 40-45 minutes longer.

Raisin Pie

Makes 1 9" pie

Raisin pie was not on the weekly menu. "We had to buy the raisins. It just wasn't as common as cherry because we grew our own cherries."

In contrast to some groups of Germanic heritage, the Lancaster Amish of this century do not—and have no memory of—serving raisin pie at their funerals. "We often have stewed prunes, but raisin pies are not a funeral tradition," said a minister's wife, whose explanation was corroborated by several others of varying ages.

The most traditional pie is one in which the raisins are stewed in water. The raisin water is then thickened. Amish cooks also sometimes make a raisin cream pie to which milk is added.

2 cups raisins	¼ tsp. salt
2 cups cold water	4 Tbsp. melted butter
1½ cups sugar	1 Tbsp. vinegar or lemon juice
4 Tbsp. flour	1 9" baked pie shell
2 eggs, separated	

In saucepan combine raisins, 1½ cups water and 1 cup sugar and bring to a boil. Combine the remaining ½ cup water and ½ cup sugar, plus flour, egg yolks, and salt; add to raisin mixture. Cook until thickened, stirring constantly. Remove from heat and add butter and vinegar or lemon juice.

Pour mixture into baked pie shell. Cover with whipped cream or meringue.

Meringue

Beat egg whites till stiff peaks form. Gradually add 2 Tbsp. sugar while beating. Pile on top of pie and bake at 350° till golden brown, about 10 minutes.

Old-Fashioned Crumb Cake

Makes 1 long cake or 2 round cakes

A moist coffee cake that is enhanced when eaten with applesauce, peaches, or pears. It needs no icing.

3 cups flour
2 cups brown sugar
½ cup shortening, butter, or margarine
1 egg, beaten

1 cup buttermilk
1 tsp. baking soda
1 tsp. cream of tartar

Mix flour and brown sugar together. Cut in shortening until mixture is crumbly. Take out 1 cup crumbs for topping.

Add to remaining crumbs the egg, buttermilk, soda, and cream of tartar, in that order. Mix well after each addition.

Pour into a greased 9" x 13" baking pan or two pie plates or cake pans. Sprinkle reserved cup of crumbs over top. Bake at 375° for 25-30 minutes.

Oatmeal Cake

Makes 1 9" x 13" cake

A moist cake, compatible with fresh or canned fruit.

1 cup rolled oats	1 tsp. baking soda
1¼ cups boiling water	½ tsp. salt
½ cup butter or margarine	1 tsp. cinnamon
1 cup granulated sugar	1⅔ cup flour
1 cup brown sugar	1 tsp. vanilla
2 eggs	

Mix oats and boiling water together; set aside for 20 minutes.

Cream butter or margarine and sugars together thoroughly. Add eggs, one at a time, beating well after each one. Blend in oatmeal mixture.

Sift together remaining dry ingredients. Fold into batter. Stir in vanilla.

Pour into a greased and floured 9" x 13" baking pan. Bake at 350° for 30-35 minutes.

After baking, but before the cake cools, spread the following topping over it and broil about 2 minutes or until it browns. Watch carefully since it burns easily!

Topping

6 Tbsp. butter or margarine, melted	1 cup brown sugar
¼ cup milk or cream	½ cup nuts, chopped

Mix together thoroughly.

Sour Cream Sugar Cookies

Sugar cookies' plain looks belie the emotion that sugar-cookie connoisseurs carry for them.

"Our favorites were sugar cookies with a little confectioner's sugar sprinkled on top."

"We ate lots of sugar cookies, sometimes with a little lemon in the batter."

"We made our batter with sour cream, rolled out the dough, and put a raisin on top of each."

"I can't make them like my mother, who used buttermilk!"

"I make drop sugar cookies, but my mother made rolled ones. Hers were spongy soft. When they're rolled and cut out, they rise to the same height all over."

1½ cups sugar	3¾ cups flour
1 cup margarine	2 tsp. baking powder
2 eggs	1 tsp. soda
1 cup sour cream or buttermilk	1 tsp. vanilla

Cream sugar and shortening. Add eggs and beat well.

Add milk, dry ingredients, and vanilla and mix thoroughly.

Drop by teaspoonsful onto greased cookie sheet. Bake at 375° for 8-10 minutes.

Variation: Use 1 tsp. lemon extract in place of vanilla.

Place a raisin in the center and sprinkle the top of each cookie with sugar before baking.

Molasses Cookies

Makes 8 dozen cookies

Molasses cookies, along with sugar cookies, top the list of fondly remembered old favorites. Molasses was a commonly used sweetener in the 19th century when refined sugar was at a premium in the New World.

Today's molasses cookies also call for sugar, but they retain the sturdy, cakey quality that has always made them loved.

Variations abound from household to household.

"We ate molasses spice."

"Ours were fat molasses cookies."

"We had soft molasses cakes with icing."

1 cup shortening	1 pint buttermilk
½ lb. light brown sugar	6 cups flour
1 pint dark baking molasses	1 Tbsp. baking soda

Cream shortening and sugar. Add molasses and buttermilk.

Stir in flour and baking soda.

Drop in large dollops from teaspoon onto cookie sheet. Bake at 375° for 8-10 minutes.

Variation: Cookies may be glazed by brushing tops with egg yolks before baking.
  Add 1 tsp. ginger and 1 tsp. cinnamon with flour and soda.

Whoopie Pies

Makes 4 dozen sandwich pies

These cookies are a relatively new invention, first appearing about 30-35 years ago. Said one grandmother in her mid-50s, "I don't remember whoopie pies as a little girl, but I do know they were around before we were married. Probably someone just made them up!"

Another grandmother in her late 50s knew of them "just since we're married, and that not in the first years."

These individual cakes are well suited to lunch-box travel and food stands at farm sales. The icing is spread between the two cookie halves so it doesn't rub off when wrapped, as cupcake icing does.

The original—and still most commonly made—whoopie pie is chocolate. Oatmeal and pumpkin variations have developed more recently.

2 cups sugar	2 tsp. vanilla
1 cup shortening	1 tsp. salt
2 eggs	1 cup sour milk
4 cups flour	2 tsp. baking soda
1 cup baking cocoa	1 cup hot water

Cream sugar and shortening. Add eggs.

Sift together flour, cocoa, and salt. Add to creamed mixture alternately with sour milk. Add vanilla.

Dissolve soda in hot water and add last. Mix well.

Drop by rounded teaspoonful onto cookie sheet. Bake at 400° for 8-10 minutes.

Make sandwiches from 2 cookies filled with Whoopie Pie Filling.

Filling

2 egg whites, beaten	4 cups 10x sugar
4 Tbsp. milk	1½ cups shortening
2 tsp. vanilla	

Mix together egg whites, milk, vanilla and 2 cups 10x sugar. Then beat in shortening and remaining 2 cups of 10x sugar.

Spread dab of filling on flat side of cooled cookie. Top with another cookie to form a sandwich pie.

Kisses

Makes about 2 lbs.

Coconuts could be bought at the turn of the century in eastern Pennsylvania. They were, of course, in their hard shells, leaving it up to the enterprising cook (or her helpers) to ferret out their meat and grate it. Coconut was a delicacy in cakes, cracker puddings, and, on occasion, candy.

3 egg whites	1 tsp. vanilla
2 cups plus 1 Tbsp. sugar	2 cups flaked coconut
2 tsp. vinegar	

Beat egg whites till frothy. Gradually add sugar and vinegar. Beat until fluffy (about 10 minutes). Stir in vanilla and coconut.

Drop by teaspoons onto cookie sheets. Bake at 250° for 30-45 minutes.

Variation: Crushed nuts may be substituted for coconut.

Pinwheel Date Cookies

Makes 3½ dozen cookies

This cookie was not part of the weekly baking; it requires far too much time in preparation! But it has traditionally been part of holiday cookie-making.

1 cup shortening	4-4½ cups flour
2 cups brown sugar	1 tsp. salt
½ cup granulated sugar	1 tsp. baking soda
3 eggs	1 tsp. cinnamon

Cream together the shortening and sugar. Add the eggs and beat until fluffy.

Sift the flour; then add the salt, soda, and cinnamon and sift again. Add the dry ingredients to the creamed mixture and beat until smooth. Chill dough in the refrigerator for a few hours. Divide the chilled dough into two parts. Roll each ¼" thick and spread with filling.

Filling

1½ cups dates or raisins, ground	1 cup water
1 cup sugar	½ cup nuts, chopped fine

Combine the fruit, sugar, and water and cook until thickened, stirring constantly. Remove from heat and add the nuts. Cool and spread on the rolled dough.

Roll up, jelly-roll fashion, and chill thoroughly in the refrigerator. Slice in rings ⅛" thick and place on greased cookie sheets, 1 inch apart. Bake at 375° until golden brown.

Cracker Pudding

Makes 6-8 servings

Cracker pudding at mealtime was a pleasurable routine. It is one more way to include saltines in the diet, although their presence is scarcely distinguishable in the finished dessert.

Even 75 years ago the Amish of eastern Pennsylvania had access to coconuts. "We would buy a whole one and grate it ourselves," says an 80-plus-year-old.

2 eggs, separated
⅔ cup granulated sugar
1 quart milk
1¼-1½ cups saltine crackers,
    coarsely broken

¾ cup coconut, grated (optional)
1 tsp. vanilla
3 Tbsp. sugar

Beat eggs yolks and sugar together. Pour into saucepan and heat. Gradually add the milk, stirring constantly.

Add crackers and coconut and cook until thickened. Remove from heat and stir in vanilla.

Pour into baking dish. Add 3 Tbsp. sugar to egg whites and beat until stiffened. Spread over pudding, then brown the meringue under the broiler.

Variation: Beat the egg whites until stiff, then fold them into the pudding while it is still hot. Chill and serve.

Apple Butter in the Oven

This is, admittedly, a short-cut procedure that fits better in smaller kitchens and homesteads than the outdoor apple-butter-over-a-fire.

One woman, who grew up helping to stir the cider for hours as it boiled down, discovered this method after much experimenting.

8 quarts thick applesauce　　　　**4 cups brown sugar**
8 quarts fresh cider　　　　　　　**1 tsp. salt**

Make 8 quarts of thick applesauce. Place hot applesauce into a 400° oven.

Place cider in large kettle and boil until half has evaporated. Add cider to sauce in the oven. Allow oven door to stand slightly ajar so steam can escape. Stir occasionally.

After about 2 hours add sugar and salt. Mix well. Allow about 2 more hours of cooking time until apple butter is the desired consistency, remembering to stir occasionally. Seal in jars.

Apple Dumplings

Makes 8 servings

These individually packaged apple "pies" make a meal or a monumental dessert. They are best eaten warm with cold milk poured over.

8 apples, cored and pared	⅓ cup cold water
3 cups flour	1 Tbsp. vinegar
1 tsp. salt	½ cup margarine
1¼ cups shortening	1 cup brown sugar
1 egg, beaten	4 Tbsp. water

Mix flour and salt. Cut in shortening.

Combine egg, ⅓ cup cold water, and vinegar and stir into the shortening mixture. Let stand a few minutes.

Roll out dough on floured board and cut into squares, so that each is large enough to fit up around an apple. When an apple is completely wrapped in dough, place it in a greased 9" x 13" baking pan.

Bring margarine, brown sugar, and 4 Tbsp. water to a boil. Pour over dumplings.

Bake at 350° for 40-50 minutes or until dumplings are golden brown.

Fresh Meadow Tea

Makes ½ gallon

Multiple varieties of tea grow in meadows, gardens, and flower beds in eastern Pennsylvania. The leaves can be used fresh, dried, or frozen.

Many cooks keep a gallon jar of fresh tea in the refrigerator from May through September. They also see to it that tea leaves and stems are laid out on paper to dry in a little-used corner of the house. (It's a way to insure a supply of meadow tea for hot drinks in the wintertime.) Those with access to a freezer have discovered the convenience of mixing up a tea concentrate and freezing it for some future occasion when time or the season does not allow making it with fresh leaves.

1 cup sugar
1 pint water
1 cup fresh tea leaves,
    either peppermint or spearmint

juice of 1 lemon
water

Stir sugar and pint of water together in a saucepan and bring to a boil.

Pour boiling syrup over tea leaves and let steep for 20 minutes. Remove the leaves and let tea cool.

Add the lemon juice and enough water to make ½ gallon of tea.

Serve either hot or cold.